GREETINGS FROM ROME

Bruce Marshall

THUNDER BAY
P·R·E·S·S

San Diego, California

The Eternal City

Magnificent capital of the ancient world

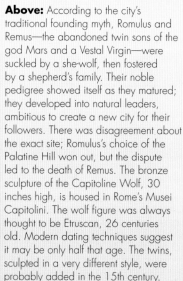

In the dark ages of European land-grabbing, the marauders and invaders were mostly (to put it mildly) uncouth gangs—the Vikings, Goths, and Huns who terrorized Britain and the Atlantic seaboard. But the powers that had designs on the Italian peninsula came from more cultivated stock the civilized democracy of Greece and the artistically inclined, democratic city-state empire of the near-eastern Etruscans.

Thus, as Rome fought off such intruders and gathered wealth and colonies, good taste and design-consciousness permeated the city's DNA. It lasts to this day, with Rome and its residents regarded as among the most stylish of all urban societies.

The location's seven hills (plus a couple of ridges) had provided lofty safety for the

Below: A major 17th-century publishing project consisted of bird's-eye prospects of more than 500 cities. Joris Hoefnagel contributed this one of Rome.

ROMA.

Above: According to the city's traditional founding myth, Romulus and Remus—the abandoned twin sons of the god Mars and a Vestal Virgin—were suckled by a she-wolf, then fostered by a shepherd's family. Their noble pedigree showed itself as they matured; they developed into natural leaders, ambitious to create a new city for their followers. There was disagreement about the exact site; Romulus's choice of the Palatine Hill won out, but the dispute led to the death of Remus. The bronze sculpture of the Capitoline Wolf, 30 inches high, is housed in Rome's Musei Capitolini. The wolf figure was always thought to be Etruscan, 26 centuries old. Modern dating techniques suggest it may be only half that age. The twins, sculpted in a very different style, were probably added in the 15th century.

for buildings in classical Greek style. Roman engineering genius fashioned them into large arches, vaults, and domes—features grander than the Greeks had imagined. Gold filigree, gilt-bronze and painted terra-cotta echoed the luxurious Etruscan legacy.

earliest settlements. They were made of the outpourings of long-extinct volcanoes and, as the city coalesced, they supplied fine materials

Left: All the gods of ancient Rome were honored in the Pantheon, under what is still the world's largest unreinforced concrete dome.

Right: The Colosseum is certainly the most visited of the ancient empire's surviving artifacts.

By about the third century AD, this was the most magnificent city on earth. "I found Rome a city of clay," Emperor Augustus said, "and left it of marble." Trade with and taxation of its colonies supported a million residents, a number London and Paris would not reach until the nineteenth century.

The prosperity was not to last, although many of the relics would. In the fourth century, Constantinople supplanted Rome as capital of the Holy Roman Empire, and at one point, the papacy decamped to Avignon in France. However, after a millennium of decline, Rome's earlier hospitality to Christianity paid off when Pope Nicolas V determined that Rome should be the permanent home of the papacy.

New riches arrived and, with them, the brilliant talents of the Renaissance.

The Seven Hills

Vantage points for the rulers of the world

The celebrated Seven Hills of Rome give gentle contours to this urban landscape. But the topography was not always so unthreatening. The earliest settlers were at pains to build up the hills and ridges as high and steep-sided as possible so their settlements were secure from marauders and the malaria-carrying mosquitoes of the low-lying plains below.

As the tiny hamlets fused into a city state, these peculiarities became increasingly inconvenient. Fortifications were torn down, tops of hills leveled, the rubble tossed into the valleys below—and the Seven Hills settled as friendly features on a stage set for

Right: Re-erected columns from the Augustan rebuild of the Temple of Apollo Sosianus.

Below: Ruins of the Palatine Hill, now an open air museum

the architectural symmetry and splendor that make Rome the most interesting antiquarian locality in the world.

The Esquiline was the largest of the hills. Nero built his Golden House here; old burial pits became the Emperor Augustus's Gardens of Maecenas. The Palatine is the central hill. Romulus lived here (Remus's stronghold was to the south, on the Aventine Hill). Caesar's assassins took refuge on the Capitoline Hill, and before the great leveling, criminals were executed by being dropped onto the crags at its base.

And so on . . . Quirinal, Viminal, Caelian. Today they are distinctive neighborhoods—quietly residential in the case of the Aventine and busily industrious around the Esquiline's showplace church, Santa Maria Maggiore.

Below: Artifacts have been saved for the Capitoline Hill's museums since the 15th century. Many are fragments, after destructions ordered by the Church.

Below: Further splendors of Capitoline Hill: the white marble Arch of Septimius Severus at its foot, and urban planning by Michelangelo—the Piazza del Campidoglio.

The Renaissance

Urban splendor that bewitched the world

The fabulously wealthy merchants and bankers of Florence were the first patrons of the artists who founded the Renaissance, the cultural explosion that launched Europe out

The Catholic Church, gathering wealth from all across Christendom, was the source of all local power and influence. And for the noble families, shows of architectural and artistic splendor demonstrated status and authority and, thus, qualification for the scarlet silks of cardinals, and even the papal tiara. (After all, people as ambitiously worldly as the Medici and Borgias

Above: A macabre tomb at Santa Maria del Popolo

of the Middle Ages. But when the papacy permanently settled in Rome, with the election of Martin V in 1417, the most munificent patronage was soon to be found there.

Above: Michelangelo thought his *Moses*, intended for a papal tomb, to be his most lifelike sculpture.

would at times rule the Holy See.)

Brilliant talents flowered under such patronage. Michelangelo (who arrived from Florence in 1496, aged twenty-one), together with Raphael, Bramante, and Perugino, built, painted, and sculpted "to the glory of God" and for the personal aggrandizement of bishops and businessmen.

For the builders, the prime influence was the classicism all around them. As confidence grew, the glorious re-creation of the city was continued in more theatrical style by Bernini and Borromini; their flamboyant work would be labeled baroque.

Right: The church of Santa Maria del Popolo. Dominating an elegant piazza, this triumph of the Renaisssance has baroque enhancements by Bernini.

Vatican City

A holy city, a state, a treasure trove

Vatican City is a sovereign state within a state and the ultimate place of pilgrimage for the world's Roman Catholics. It also displays the greatest treasures of the Renaissance—and so much more.

The entrance is a dramatic overture—Gian Lorenzo Bernini's seventeenth-century Piazza San Pietro, a fanfare of colonnaded curves surmounted by statuary, leading to the Vatican's spiritual heart, St. Peter's Basilica, universally identified by the vast dome designed by Michelangelo.

In fact all the great Renaissance and baroque artists contributed to this sumptuous temple: Donato Bramante was the architect first chosen by Pope Julius II for what was a sixteenth-century rebuilding so that Pope Julius might have a fitting setting for his own

Above: A portrait of Pope Julius II—a powerful patron

Below: Michelangelo planned the dome of St. Peter's to be "the greatest dome in Christendom." There were rivals in Florence and Rome.

Above: The view from the Dome of St. Peter's, over a concourse designed to allow the maximum number of believers observe papal blessings.

Left: Erecting the central obelisk in 1586. The red granite pillar had been brought from Egypt by Emperor Caligula.

tomb. Raphael was, for a time, director of works. Carlo Maderno designed the travertine facade; Bernini built and embellished on site for half a century.

It was Pope Julius who commissioned Michelangelo's frescoed ceiling for the nearby Sistine Chapel, scene of the Holy See's most stately ceremonies. Its massive walls are also intricately decorated, carrying twelve paintings by, among others, Botticelli and Perugino, and what is considered to be the crowning work of Michelangelo's later career—*The Last Judgement*, painted twenty years after finishing the chapel ceiling.

Left: Dominating this atrium lobby, Giuseppe Momo's 1932 spiral staircase is a double helix: a one-way route up, and one down.

Below: The 1990s restoration of Michelangelo's *The Last Judgement* removed earlier censorship, "the fig-leaf campaign."

Vatican Museums

The world's smallest state displays its fabulous wealth

Above: The Swiss Guards are, indeed, Swiss, and have been since 15th-century popes used Swiss mercenaries as bodyguards.

Left: The Stanza della Segnatura, one of four rooms decorated by Raphael and his studio, initially for Pope Julius II.

When stepping into St. Peter's Square, visitors are no longer in Italy but in the Vatican state. Thus, the trappings of sovereignty are evident with its own passports and postage stamps, TV and radio stations, a newspaper, railway system (the shortest in the world), and an army of 110 soldiers—the colorfully uniformed Swiss Guards. The territory covers 110 acres, half of it gardens, but dominated physically and philosophically by the Vatican museums,

brimming with treasures displayed in more than fifty galleries.

The buildings themselves are former palaces of popes and cardinals; the collections owe much to the acquisitiveness of those worldly prelates who, intoxicated by the creative genius of the Renaissance, sent agents scouring the known world for *ogetti di valore* (valuable objects), any *ogetti.*

Some of Italy's most important archeological finds are here, along with Greek, Egyptian, and Etruscan treasures, and masterworks of tapestry, bookmaking, and cartography. Raphael's last painting, found after his death, is a highlight of the world's most important array of Renaissance splendors. And a continuing concern for collecting is expressed in a gallery of contemporary art inaugurated by Pope Paul VI.

Above and below: A walled orchard for a 13th-century pope became a sophisticated landscape under the direction of Renaissance gardeners such as Pirro Ligorio, who built the courtyard and summer house known as the Casina di Pius IV.

Left: The priest-geographer Ignazio Danti took three years (1580-83) to depict regions of the Italian peninsula on the walls of the Gallery of Maps. Other artists painted the vaulted ceiling.

Modest Modernists

After Il Duce's posturing, respectful renewal

Italy as a nation is younger than the United States—just 150 years old in 2011. Victor Emmanuel II became king in 1871 when the peninsula's microstates united—and Rome was the obvious candidate to be the capital.

A building boom followed, to create desk space for the new bureaucratic infrastructure, but some of the finest pieces of old Rome were

Above: The squat, white Palace of the Workers. In Mussolini's grandiose fascist dream, this was a heroic, square, second colosseum.

obvious candidates to be public buildings: the President of the Republic (the country's constitutional change came in 1946) lives in a sixteenth-century papal residence, Palazzo del Quirinale; the Senate deliberates in a former de Medici residence.

The inter-wars dictator, Benito Mussolini, dwelled on an even more ancient past—Imperial Rome. His version of fascist architecture shows in the bombastic "square

Left: Richard Meier's Jubilee Church (and community center)—a millennium project aiming to bring social renewal to a nondescript suburb. The three "shells" represent the Holy Trinity.

600

450

300

150

feet

Colosseum   Pantheon   Trajan's Column   St. Peter's Basilica   Ministero Delle Finanze I   Ministero Delle Finanze II

colosseum" of the Palazzo della Civita del Lavoro in the EUR district, a development he had intended as a site for a world fair.

Since then, planners and developers have treated the ancient heritage with discretion; few modern edifices jar the views from those favored hilltop vantage points. Nevertheless, celebrated modern architects have been at work here: a mosque by Paolo Portoghesi, paid for by the Saudi government; Richard Meier's Jubilee Church in the Tor Tre Este suburb— great curving sails of white concrete and a tower for five bells; and Renzo Piano's three-hall music complex.

Most recently Zaha Hadid has been winning prizes for her MAXXI, the National Museum of XXI Century Arts, a 30,000 square foot "campus of arts and culture."

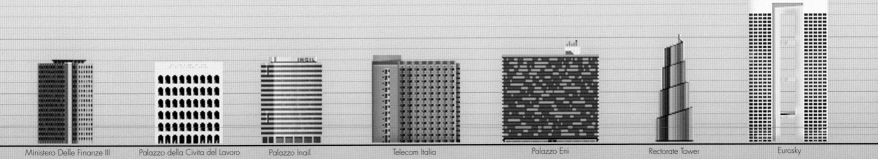

Ministero Delle Finanze III   Palazzo della Civita del Lavoro   Palazzo Inail   Telecom Italia   Palazzo Eni   Rectorate Tower   Eurosky

The Famous Fountains

A genius for working on water

Any tribute to the engineering prowess of ancient Rome begins with aqueduct admiration. While the Roman passion for channeling water brought hygiene and irrigation to an entire empire, the most sophisticated and complex constructions were in Rome itself. From source to city might be 30 miles or more, yet underground channels and overground viaducts were built with a precision that maintained a constant gradient of about 1:4,000—a half yard drop per mile.

And at journey's end there would be a public fountain—self-promotion for the ruler

Below: Coins tossed by visitors into the Trevi Fountain—worth about $4,000 a day—subsidize a charity for Rome's neediest citizens.

Above: Reclining behind a modest street fountain, Il Babuino—the baboon—is a "talking statue," identifying a wall where citizens posted satirical, critical comments on church and state.

who had commissioned the project. That sort of work went on for 500 years around the time of Christ, to be followed by centuries of vandalism and neglect. Rebuilding, in ever more spectacular extravagance, became an obsession of the Renaissance popes. That impetus led to the panoply of fountains that are a glorious feature of the modern city.

Below: Marble columns frame the Arch of Drusus—l'Arco di Druso—which supported the aqueduct serving the Baths of Caracalla.

The Fontana di Trevi is the best-known, largest, and grandest of them all, at the end of a watercourse that has served the city since 19 BC. Triton, Bernini's baroque masterpiece, shoots a jet of water 16 feet into the air, indicating its valley location and the elevation of its source. (Trevi's supply, on the other hand, arrives as a trickle; it's the ingenuity of the architect, Nicola Salvi, that creates cascading theatricality.)

Monumental, ornamental, and modestly practical—Rome has 3,000 fountains in one or other of those forms, many of the smaller ones in shaded alleys and private courtyards.

Right: Four river gods surmount Bernini's fountain in the Piazza Navona. They represent great rivers in the four continents then acknowledging papal authority.

Below: Two millennia ago, the Aqua Claudia carried enough water to serve all Rome. This remnant is in the Parco del Acquedotti.

Piazzas and Parks

Room to breathe, space to relax

Rome caters for its residents' downtime with two universally admired features—piazzas and parks—which, all across the city, are consistently remarkable for their aura of elegance.

The piazzas—where strolling, people-watching, and coffee-sipping slow the pace of city-dwelling—wear layers of history. None more so than the Piazza Navona, which has the oval shape of the chariot racetrack that it once was, and still wears baroque dressing by

Below: Elegant ionic columns identify the Temple of Aesculapius, named for the god of healing, overlooking a Villa Borghese lake.

Below: The Piazza di Siena in Villa Borghese park. This garden, much admired since the early 17th century, assumed its naturalist English landscaping 200 years later.

Above: Detail from a fountain in Villa Borghese park

two of the style's masters—Bernini and his pupil Borromini. Despite the nobility of the setting, there is day and night informality here, and always some amiable street drama. And just a stroll away, "the world's meeting place,"

Below: One of Europe's most celebrated urban views—the Spanish Steps seen from the Piazza di Spagna. The fountain is by Bernini Senior.

the Spanish Steps of the Piazza di Spagna, overlooked by the twin bell towers of Trinita dei Monte.

From the church's front steps, there are views across Rome; such vantage points are treasured by Romans, who enjoy them particularly from the gardens that give the city

Above: The palace of the Pamphili family overlooked the Piazza Navona—a family once powerful enough to be allowed to flood the square for aquatic summer celebrations.

a higher proportion of green space than any other European capital. The Janiculum hill has one such garden—a park of fountains, arches, and monuments, including a lighthouse, offering a panorama of the whole city.

Most of these gardens are the former estates of churchmen and aristocrats, following a style set in the early seventeenth century at the Villa Borghese, the home of Cardinal Scipione Borghese, nephew of Pope Paul V. Hundreds of what became the city's signature tree, the Umbrella Pine, were planted in these 140 acres. Bernini's father created garden sculptures. Since the Villa Borghese became state property, museums, galleries, and academies have been introduced to the park, along with child-friendly features like a boating lake.

Buon Appetito

Celebrating the good ingredients

Those hedonistic prelates of the sixteenth century competed at hospitable entertaining as well as palace building. Pope Pius IV's chef was able to write a cookbook containing 1,000 recipes, among which stuffed peacock was one of the dishes intended more to impress than to nourish. Italy enjoyed Europe's leading food culture; the chefs that Catherine de Medici took to France on her marriage with Henry II instituted French *haute cuisine*.

Modern Romans take a less fancy view, celebrating local, seasonal ingredients, taking care to enhance their natural flavors, not disguise, and aiming to have them on the table within hours/days of harvesting, not weeks.

If there's a throwback to ancient tradition,

Above: In the morning, the Campo dei Fiori is a market laden with fresh produce, accompanied by the fragrance from bread and pizza ovens. Later in the day, it becomes a bustling wining, dining, and entertainment center.

Left: Blackboard presentation emphasizes the informality of Roman hospitality. Bruschette are snacks—roasted bread, rubbed with garlic, drizzled with olive oil, and tastily topped.

Above: Roman fascination with food is not a new phenomenon, as this mosaic in a Vatican museum demonstrates.

it is to the humble habits of the Jewish ghetto; *alla giuda*—in the Jewish style—is a common restaurant description of dishes whose modest ingredients have been enlivened with the spices once known only in kosher households. And some domestic kitchens still acknowledge an ancient routine—gnocchi on Thursday, *baccala* (salt cod) or seafood on Friday, and tripe or sweetbreads on Saturday.

Highlights of the Roman *campagna's* abundance are globe artichokes and fava beans, goat and milk-fed lamb, pecorino sheep's cheese, and pork lard preserved for the winter . . . all to be found at the lively Campo dei Fiori, one of Europe's greatest open air food markets.

Or there are the cool delicatessens hung with hams and salamis, salt cod, and garlic, whose patrons seem anxious to try a tiny taste of everything on display. These are the campaigners for the burgeoning international Slow Food movement, which was founded in Rome when an American fast food chain first threatened the Piazza di Spagna.

Above: High flavor at high speed—classic saltimbocca consists of veal slices, prosciutto, and sage, quickly sautéed.

Left: The Roman food scene. The dishes here feature favorite local ingredients: truffles and mushrooms, penne pasta (above); and artichoke, deep-fried in the traditional Jewish manner.

Treats on the Streets

Coffee, cake, and cold, cold comfort

Bucket-sized paper cups are *not* the vessels for serving coffee in Rome. The regular Roman starts the day with a shot of espresso, standing at a café's bar (it's twice as expensive sitting down). If there's real need for a heart-starter, the order might be for a ristretto, a thimble-full, twice as strong, which depends for its stimulating effect on the finest beans being precisely roasted and particularly finely ground.

A frothy cappuccino is for mid-morning—

Above: Elektra Belle Epoque espresso machine

never after dinner in the American manner. If black coffee needs an assist late in the day, it will be a corretto, "corrected" with a shot of grappa.

The myriad bars will serve cakes (dolci) and maybe ice cream (gelato), but there are also dedicated temples, known as gelateria, that offer samples of the most delicious of Italian specialties. And for these treats, one must sit down, preferably outside, with a Renaissance facade across the street as backdrop to the easy elegance of Rome. The sweet indulgence might be a simple nibble—an amaretto biscuit dunked in sweet wine, *vin santo*. Or the more ambitious maritozzi, a sugary croissantlike

Above: Cakes in a Roman pasticceria

Below: During summer evenings, the gelateria is the busiest shop in town as people choose from the huge variety of flavors.

bun filled with cream. Or a crostata di ricotta, particularly Roman, the noblest specimen of cheesecake.

At the gelateria, decision-making may become more subtle and serious. Whose coffee for your coffee ice cream—Jamaica's, Java's, Costa Rica's? Forty percent cocoa for your chocolate cornetto, or 70 percent? An ice cream served in a warm bun? Brave enough to try fennel and licorice?

Some of these shrines date back to the nineteenth century, like Fassi, near Termini Station, which claims to be Italy's oldest and largest gelateria. Giolitti, near the Pantheon, has the high ceilings and mirrors and marble of that time. Oddly, traditional ideas have given the trade a new lease of life, under the influence of the Slow Food movement: the sign Gelaterie Artigianale indicates a return to the old days of only fresh ingredients, no artificial colors or flavors.

Left and below: Café society thrives in Rome, with sidewalk seating seeming to line every street. The locals, however, stand up for their coffee, as at the Caffè Farnese. In winter, hot chocolate is the choice for leisurely, convivial drinking.

Above: Where there isn't a café, there will be a mobile source of cool drinks and ices.

Movie Memories

Behind the camera and in shot, the city stars

Ancient Rome has provided many backdrops for the daring acts of Hollywood heroes, as gory gladiators, fearsome warrior-slaves, daredevil charioteers. Think *Gladiator, Spartacus, Ben-Hur*. But more amiable exploits, set in the modern city, are likely to stay longer in the movie memory: Audrey Hepburn and Gregory Peck aboard a scooter in *Roman Holiday*; Anita Ekberg fountain-dunking in *La Dolce Vita*, the

1960 masterwork by Federico Fellini.

Fellini practiced his trade at the Cinecitta, Europe's biggest film production complex—a 100-acre spread six miles from the city center, built in the 1930s when Mussolini recognized film as the most potent propaganda vehicle of the time. In the aftermath of World War II,

Right: A set for Martin Scorcese's Gangs of New York, re-creates Broadway at the Cinecitta film production facility.

Below: Charlton Heston is Ben-Hur in one of Hollywood's many attempts to portray the gory glories of Ancient Rome.

Above: A Lifetime Achievement Oscar recognized Federico Fellini's contribution to movie-making. His *La Dolce Vita* of 1960 (left) is considered one of the all-time great films, a profound influence on later writers and directors.

those facilities were severely limited, leading to Italy's most important contribution to the art of the film—neorealism, as practiced by Roberto Rosselini and Vittorio de Sica, whose *Bicycle Thieves* featured amateur actors in miserable (and free) Roman locations.

But when Cinecitta recovered from its war wounds—German armies had looted it as they retreated north—Fellini made it his creative home and inspired a golden age of Italian movie making. Hollywood, too, decamped here, exploiting cheaper facilities, although for a while gossip rather than artistic achievement grabbed the attention. It was at Cinecitta that Elizabeth Taylor, arriving to play Cleopatra, met Richard Burton and began that tempestuous real-life love story.

Right: The rain and squalor of Bicycle Thieves—that was the Rome of the neorealist filmmakers. But the stars also came out: Anita Ekberg (*La Dolce Vita*), Audrey Hepburn and Gregory Peck (*Roman Holiday*), and Rex Harrison and Elizabeth Taylor (*Cleopatra*).

Dramatic Settings

Where all the city's a stage

Rome has concert halls and theaters befitting the high quality of its lively arts, but the city plays to other distinctive strengths—charismatic locations and Mediterranean summer weather—to enhance the drama. The appeal of sacred music soars when the source is the transept of a Renaissance church; performance under the stars adds credibility to even the most unlikely operatic plots.

There's surely no grander setting for church music than the vast basilica of St. Peter's, and Rome residents join the Pope himself there for a regular, televised December concert. Plainsong and Gregorian chant are to be heard at the Benedictine church of Sant' Anselmo. And throughout the city, choirs with local allegiances tune up for the Easter and Christmas festivals, notably the singing of the *Te Deum* at Gesù, Rome's first Jesuit church.

Right: Tosca, set in Rome, premiered in Rome—in 1900.

Above: Music to celebrate 150 years of Italian unity

But then, come June, performers of all kinds come out to play. Church cloisters, palace courtyards, the gardens of the great villas become the stages for music and opera, theater, and dance. Most dramatic of all the outdoor settings, the ruins of the Baths of Caracalla, and even—if there's a superstar in town, pop or serious—the Colosseum where ancient Romans once enjoyed their more macabre entertainments.

Right: Music and drama in spectacular settings—opera at the Caracalla Baths (top left), a "sound and light" show at the Villa Borghese (top right), and (bottom) the Abruzzo Symphony Orchestra plays for charity in the Colosseum.

Style for Sale

Highlighting new fashion and old treasures

Rome ranks fourth, after Paris, New York, and Milan, as a fashion capital. Famous names such as Bulgari and Brioni had their founding ateliers here, priming a neighborhood now devoted to retail therapy. The Via Condotti, at the foot of the Spanish steps, bustling, shaded, intimate, is at the heart of it—a neat crisscross of streets known, somewhat inelegantly, as the Quadrilateral Area.

But there's little that's inelegant about the glittering window displays here, patrolled by respectful fashionistas and fascinated tourists.

Right and below: Vuitton, Armani, Prada . . . three great fashion brands that are not native to Rome—but the pursuit of prestige requires a presence here. Furthermore, business can boom: store security is often required to limit the number of eager shoppers crowding through the doors.

ANTICHITA

1872

Antique dealers provide punctuation points—showing equally elegant but less ephemeral treasures.

And antiquarians have other citadels: there are thirty or so prestigious dealers around the Via del Babuino, twenty more on the Via Giulia, near the Campo dei Fiori market square. The Via dei Coronari is lined with showrooms, and is home to an annual antiques fair when the nighttime street is lit by torches.

All this, however, is serious, heavy-duty trade. The visitor seeking a portable, affordable souvenir might head for the Porta Portese Sunday flea market. The bargaining starts at 6:30 am; the ritual technique is to offer half the asking price.

Right: Window gazers admire Via Condotti displays.

Below: Eclectic bargains at the Porta Portese market

Rome Versus Rome

The soccer rivalry that divides a city

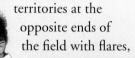

Soccer (the word is an American usage, derived from Association Football) is faraway the most popular sport in Italy, and Rome has two teams in Serie A, the top tier of competition, SS Lazio, who play in sky blue and white, and AS Roma, in maroon and gold. They share a home ground, the Stadio Olimpico, and when they meet there—a fixture known as the *Derby della Capitale*—fireworks are as likely in the stands as on the field. The rivalry dates from the days of Mussolini, when Lazio defied *Il Duce's* plan to merge all the local teams into one strong enough to challenge the dominant northern clubs of Turin and Milan.

Today, the notorious Ultras, particularly fanatical fans with allegiances to clubs across Europe, set the pace and style of support for the two Roman clubs by marking their territories at the opposite ends of the field with flares,

Above: Roma are known to their supporters as I Giallorossi—the Yellow-Reds.

Below: The Stadio Olimpico, where Roma's striker Francesco Totti (foreground, right) is a local hero.

flags, and banners. On a good day, it's a noisy, colorful, amiable show; the occasional bad one descends into violence and chanted hatred. On the field, AS Roma had the best of the 2010–11 season, winning all three derbies.

The Stadio Olimpico is part of the Foro Italico sports complex, a 1930s project for the architects, Enrico Del Debbio and Luigi Moretti—favorites of Mussolini. Thus it reflects the dictator's obsession with the

Below: Fans celebrate Italy's victory in the 2006 World Cup—the game's most prestigious tournament.

S.S.LAZIO

Right: Marble figures overlooking the Stadio dei Marmi express Mussolini's vision of athleticism.

Left: Lazio's badge leads to their nickname—Aqualotti, the Young Eagles.

imperial age: the Stadio dei Marmi's marble steps are lined with more than fifty classical-style statues of athletes. The Foro also hosts international competitions in tennis and swimming.

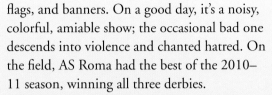

Wish You Were Here

La Dolce Vita, saintly and secular

All roads lead to Rome, they say—or, rather, said, when it was the most powerful city state on Earth. The physical remnants of that mighty metropolis survive to a remarkable degree, and roads to Rome now throng with visitors who come to honor a stone and marble heritage preserved by the Mediterranean climate for two millennia.

In years of holy significance to Roman Catholics, when the Vatican becomes a place of pilgrimage, the number of visitors may be double the norm, making Rome, briefly and intermittently, the world's most visited city.

Right: The postcards celebrate the city's Roman Catholic heritage, and also more pagan gods from the distant past.

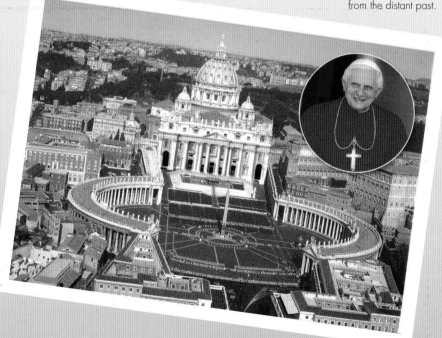

Cappella Sistina — Funerali di S. S. Pio X.

The Colosseum, Rome
© Corbis

POST CARD

PLACE
STAMP
HERE

_____

_____

_____

_____

Monument to King Victor Emmanuel II, Rome
© Corbis

POST CARD

PLACE
STAMP
HERE

_____

_____

_____

_____

St. Peter's Basilica and the Tiber River, Rome
© Corbis

POST CARD

PLACE
STAMP
HERE

_____

_____

_____

_____

Barcaccia Fountain and Spanish Steps, Rome
© Corbis

POST CARD

PLACE
STAMP
HERE

_____

_____

_____

_____